Pebble® Plus

Women in Sports

MICHELLE WIE

by Mary Dunn

CAPSTONE PRESS
a capstone imprint

Pebble Plus is published by Capstone Press
1710 Roe Crest Drive, North Mankato, Minnesota 56003
www.mycapstone.com

Library of Congress Cataloging-in-Publication Data
Cataloging-in-Publication Data is on file with the Library of Congress.
ISBN 978-1-4914-7976-6 (library binding)
ISBN 978-1-4914-8572-9 (paperback)
ISBN 978-1-4914-8578-1 (eBook PDF)

Editorial Credits
Abby Colich, editor; Sarah Bennett, designer; Eric Gohl, media researcher;
Katy LaVigne, production specialist

Photo Credits
Dreamstime: Chatchai Somwat, 5; Getty Images: Jamie Squire, 9, Kevin C. Cox, 17;
Newscom: ABACA/Lionel Hahn, 15, Ai Wire Photo Service/Rich Kane, 11, Kyodo,
21, Reuters/Jeff Haynes, 7, Reuters/John Sommers II, 13; Shutterstock: cjmac, cover
(background), 1, Maxene Huiyu, 19, Mega Pixel, 3, 23, NikolayN, 2, 24, Pal2iyawit,
cover, vorakorn, back cover, 11 (background), 21 (background), 22

Note to Parents and Teachers

The Women in Sports set supports national curriculum standards for social
studies related to people, places, and culture. This book describes and
illustrates Michelle Wie. The images support early readers in understanding
the text. The repetition of words and phrases helps early readers learn new
words. This book also introduces early readers to subject-specific vocabulary
words, which are defined in the Glossary section. Early readers may need
assistance to read some words and to use the Table of Contents, Glossary,
Read More, Internet Sites, Critical Thinking Using the Common Core, and
Index sections of the book.

Printed in the United States of America in North Mankato, Minnesota.
092015 009221CGS16

Table of Contents

Golfing with Family

Michelle Wie was born
October 11, 1989. Her parents
were from South Korea.
They both played golf. By age 4
Michelle was learning the sport.

TIMELINE

1989

born in
Honolulu, Hawaii

Michelle often beat her parents at golf. Her father found her a coach. Michelle worked hard. She practiced the game after every lesson.

TIMELINE

1989

born in
Honolulu, Hawaii

Amateur Golfing

In 2000 Michelle played in seven amateur tournaments. She won five of them. Michelle was the youngest amateur golfer in the USGA. Her father was often her caddy.

USGA stands for United States Golf Association.

TIMELINE

1989
born in Honolulu, Hawaii

2000
wins five of seven amateur tournaments

Michelle was tall and strong.

People called her "Big Wiesy."

Michelle could swing the club hard.

She could drive the ball far.

She won the Hawaii State

Women's Open in 2002.

TIMELINE

1989	2000	2002
born in Honolulu, Hawaii	wins five of seven amateur tournaments	wins the Hawaii State Women's Open

In 2003 Michelle won the Women's

Amateur Public Links Championship.

She was the youngest person ever

to win. In 2005 she became

the first female in a USGA

amateur men's tournament.

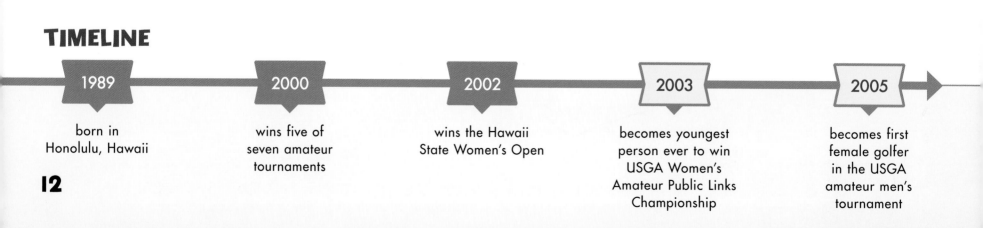

TIMELINE

1989	2000	2002	2003	2005
born in Honolulu, Hawaii	wins five of seven amateur tournaments	wins the Hawaii State Women's Open	becomes youngest person ever to win USGA Women's Amateur Public Links Championship	becomes first female golfer in the USGA amateur men's tournament

Playing as a Pro

Near her sixteenth birthday, Michelle turned pro. She began playing the best men and women golfers. Michelle was also finishing high school. She started at Stanford University in 2007.

TIMELINE

1989	2000	2002	2003	2005
born in Honolulu, Hawaii	wins five of seven amateur tournaments	wins the Hawaii State Women's Open	becomes youngest person ever to win USGA Women's Amateur Public Links Championship	becomes first female golfer in the USGA amateur men's tournament

2006

turns pro

2007

begins Stanford
University

In 2009 Michelle won
her first LPGA tournament.
In 2010 she was the top
player at the Canadian
Women's Open.

LPGA stands for Ladies
Professional Golf Association.

TIMELINE

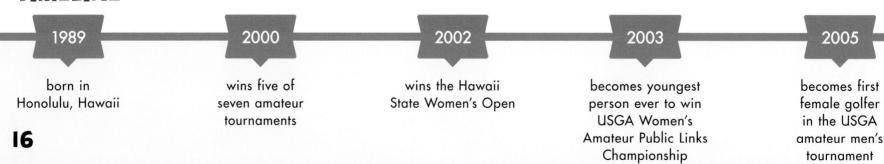

1989	2000	2002	2003	2005
born in Honolulu, Hawaii	wins five of seven amateur tournaments	wins the Hawaii State Women's Open	becomes youngest person ever to win USGA Women's Amateur Public Links Championship	becomes first female golfer in the USGA amateur men's tournament

| 2006 | 2007 | 2009 | 2010 |
| turns pro | begins Stanford University | wins first LPGA tournament | wins Canadian Women's Open |

By 2013 Michelle had four
big wins. But she still found
ways to improve. Michelle made
changes to her putting. She worked
to make her game the best.

TIMELINE

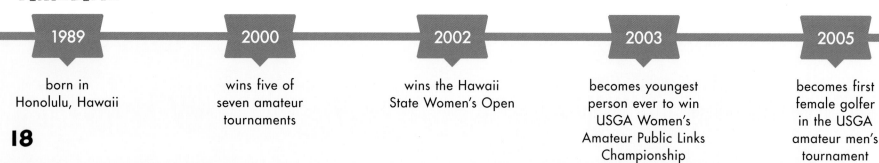

1989
born in
Honolulu, Hawaii

2000
wins five of
seven amateur
tournaments

2002
wins the Hawaii
State Women's Open

2003
becomes youngest
person ever to win
USGA Women's
Amateur Public Links
Championship

2005
becomes first
female golfer
in the USGA
amateur men's
tournament

2006

turns pro

2007

begins Stanford
University

2009

wins first
LPGA tournament

2010

wins Canadian
Women's Open

Michelle won the U.S.

Women's Open in 2014.

It was her first major title.

Michelle's hard work helps her be

one of the top female golfers.

TIMELINE

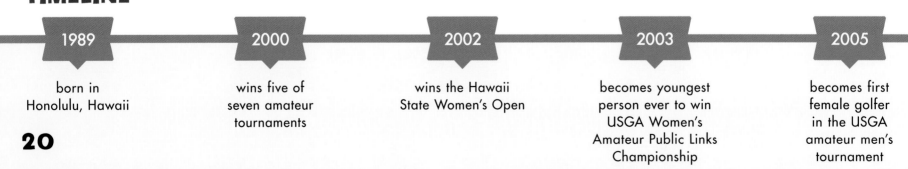

1989	2000	2002	2003	2005
born in Honolulu, Hawaii	wins five of seven amateur tournaments	wins the Hawaii State Women's Open	becomes youngest person ever to win USGA Women's Amateur Public Links Championship	becomes first female golfer in the USGA amateur men's tournament

2006	2007	2009	2010	2014
turns pro	begins Stanford University	wins first LPGA tournament	wins Canadian Women's Open	wins the U.S. Women's Open

Glossary

amateur—a person who is learning a skill

caddy—a person who carries a golfer's clubs

championship—a contest held to find a winner

drive—to hit with force

pro—short for professional; a person paid for an activity or sport

putt—a golf stroke when the ball is near the hole

title—an award given to the winner of a tournament

tournament—a series of games between several players, ending in one winner

Read More

Bates, Greg. *Michelle Wie: Golf Superstar.* Playmakers. Minneapolis: ABDO Publishing, 2016.

Hudson, Maryann. *Girls' Golf.* Girls' SportsZone. Minneapolis: ABDO Publishing, 2014.

Kawa, Katie. *Women in Sports.* Women Groundbreakers. New York: PowerKids Press, 2015.

Internet Sites

FactHound offers a safe, fun way to find Internet sites related to this book. All of the sites on FactHound have been researched by our staff.

Here's all you do:
Visit *www.facthound.com*
Type in this code: 9781491479766

Super-cool stuff! Check out projects, games and lots more at **www.capstonekids.com**

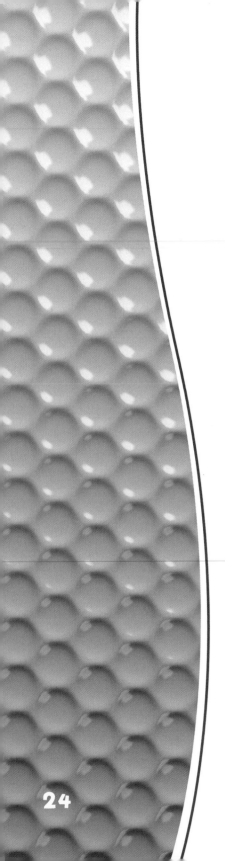

Critical Thinking
Using the Common Core

1. Reread the text on page 10. How did being tall and strong help Michelle as a golfer? (Integration of Knowledge and Ideas)

2. Reread the text on page 20. Then look at the photo on page 21. What is Michelle holding? (Craft and Structure)

Index